Super Exp

ASTRONAUTS & SPACE

Tamara Hartson

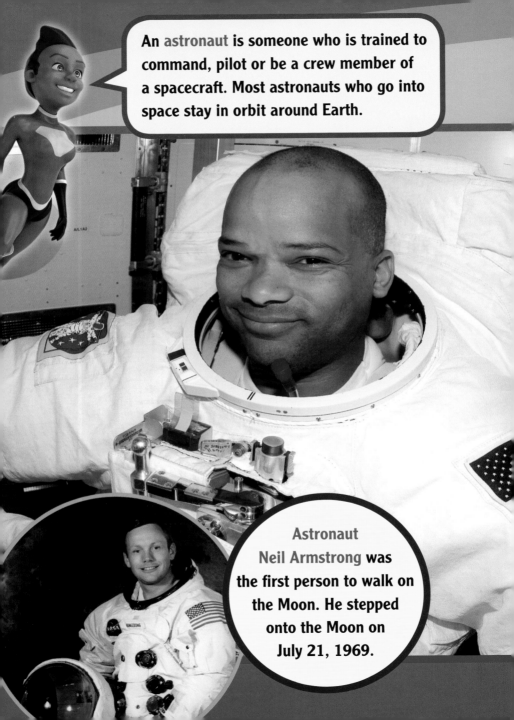

An astronaut is someone who is trained to command, pilot or be a crew member of a spacecraft. Most astronauts who go into space stay in orbit around Earth.

Astronaut Neil Armstrong was the first person to walk on the Moon. He stepped onto the Moon on July 21, 1969.

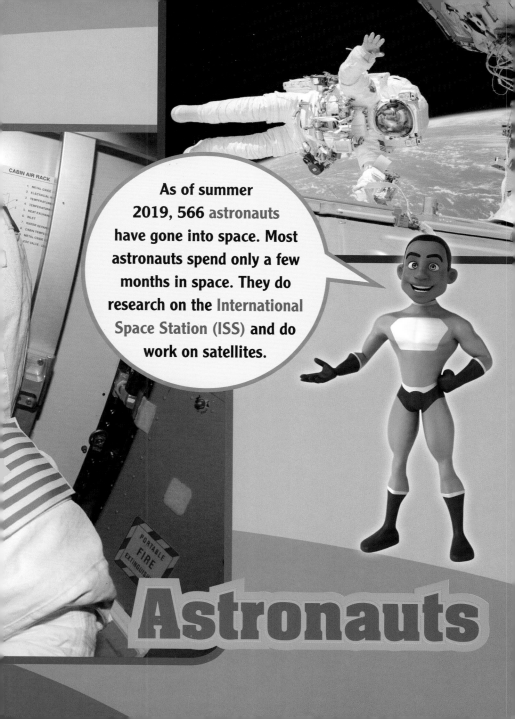

As of summer 2019, 566 astronauts have gone into space. Most astronauts spend only a few months in space. They do research on the International Space Station (ISS) and do work on satellites.

Astronauts

Space

Space is sometimes called outer space. It is the dark and starry place beyond Earth. The planet Earth is in space, just like the Sun and the Moon.

Even though space looks like it is full of stars, it is really quite empty. Stars in space are very far apart.

Many interesting things are found in space, such as planets, stars, galaxies, nebulas, asteroids and comets. In space there are also satellites and space garbage that orbit Earth.

Gravity and Microgravity

Gravity is a force that pulls objects together.
Larger objects have more of this force. Gravity
is what keeps us on Earth and the reason why
objects fall. Rain falls to Earth because of gravity.

In space, gravity is weak, so it is called microgravity. "Micro" means tiny and refers to the small effects of gravity in space. Microgravity means that astronauts in space feel weightless. The experience is sometimes called zero-gravity or zero-g.

Mission: Space

Belka

The first living beings to go into space were not humans! The Russian spacecraft Korabl-Sputnik 2 had a crew of 2 dogs, 1 rabbit, 42 mice, 2 rats, flies and several plants. All these creatures came back to Earth successfully.

The 2 dogs were both female. Their names were Belka and Strelka. After returning to Earth, Strelka later had 6 puppies. Her puppies also had puppies, and her descendents are still alive today.

Strelka

The First Astronaut

Russia was the first country in the world to send humans into space. Russian astronauts are sometimes called cosmonauts. Yuri Gagarin was the first cosmonaut to go into space and orbit the Earth.

The first Russian cosmonaut traveled inside a spherical spacecraft named the Vostok. The Vostok was attached to a rocket and launched into space. After making a full orbit of Earth, the Vostok capsule descended through the atmosphere. Yuri ejected and parachuted safely to the ground.

Project Mercury

The United States was the second country to send an astronaut into space. **NASA (National Aeronautics and Space Administration)** was formed in 1958, and its first space program was called Project Mercury. The goal was to send a small, single-person spacecraft into orbit around Earth, using a large rocket.

Spacecraft

Rocket

After several test flights, John Glenn became the first American in space. He orbited the Earth three times in a spacecraft called Friendship 7.

John Glenn

Friendship 7

Project Gemini

NASA's second space program was called Project Gemini. The United States had plans to send astronauts to the moon. Project Gemini was the program NASA used to practice space travel skills before attempting a trip to the moon.

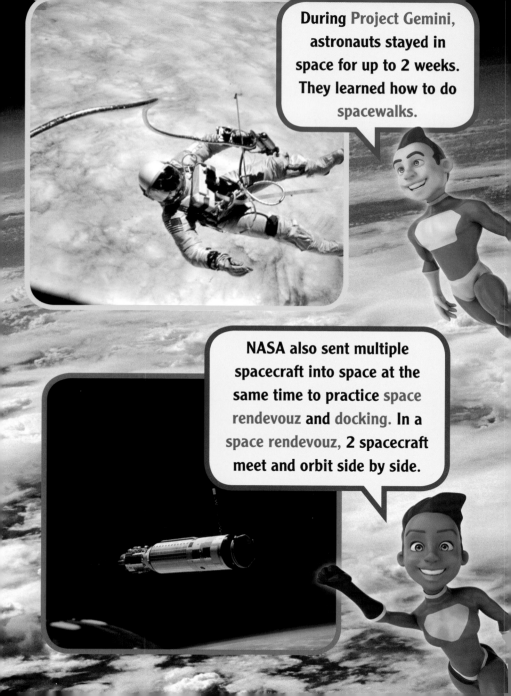

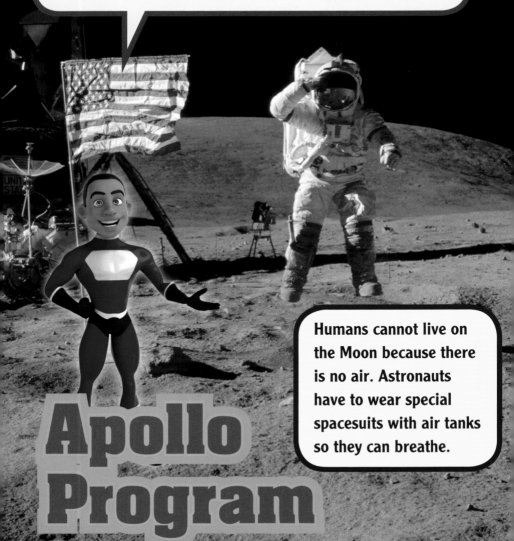

People have made 9 trips to the Moon. Each trip was called an Apollo Mission. In total, 12 astronauts have walked on the Moon. The Moon has less gravity than Earth, so walking on the Moon is like bouncing very slowly. On the moon, you could easily jump as high as a 6-storey buiding!

Humans cannot live on the Moon because there is no air. Astronauts have to wear special spacesuits with air tanks so they can breathe.

Apollo Program

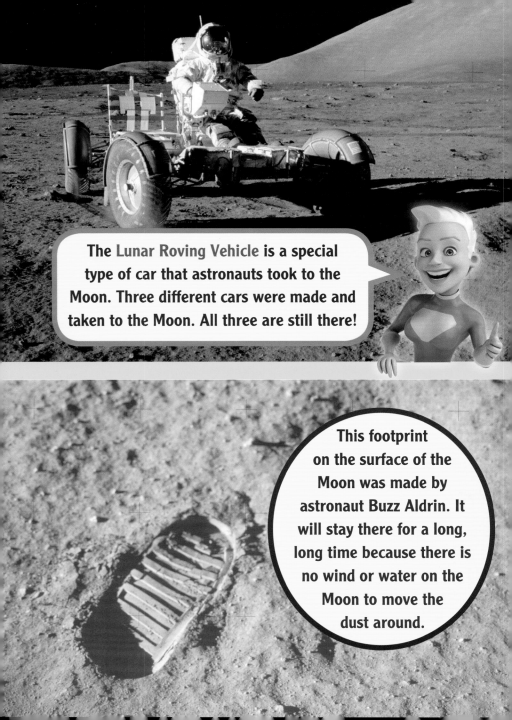

The Lunar Roving Vehicle is a special type of car that astronauts took to the Moon. Three different cars were made and taken to the Moon. All three are still there!

This footprint on the surface of the Moon was made by astronaut Buzz Aldrin. It will stay there for a long, long time because there is no wind or water on the Moon to move the dust around.

Space Shuttle

Space shuttles were designed to be used many times to take people and materials into orbit. Space shuttles were used to build the ISS.
A shuttle has 4 to 7 astronauts on board. In 30 years, five different space shuttles made 135 flights into space with 355 astronauts!

Because the shuttle is a glider, it had to be carried to the launch site on the back of a plane!

While in orbit, the doors on the back of the shuttle open to release equipment and cool the shuttle.

Becoming an astronaut is a lot of work! Astronauts must know a lot about mathematics, physics, astronomy and other science topics. Most astronauts study for many years before they even start astronaut training. Once they are accepted into training, they still have to write many exams!

Training to be an Astronaut

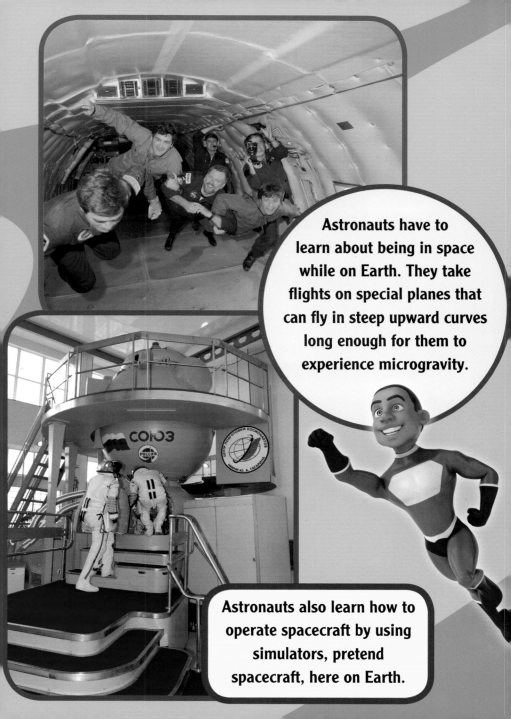

Astronauts have to learn about being in space while on Earth. They take flights on special planes that can fly in steep upward curves long enough for them to experience microgravity.

Astronauts also learn how to operate spacecraft by using simulators, pretend spacecraft, here on Earth.

Astronauts sometimes train underwater while wearing their spacesuits. This helps them get used to how it will feel to do spacewalks, called Extravehicular Activities (EVAs). Astronauts go on spacewalks outside their spacecraft to perform maintenance and other tasks.

Training Underwater

Moving underwater is not exactly the same as moving in space, but it does help astronauts get used to working and moving in their spacesuits. They have to practice working with and repairing the equipment while underwater.

International Space Station

The **International Space Station (ISS) is like** a research station in space. Astronauts from many countries travel to the **ISS** in spacecraft. America, Russia, Europe, Japan and Canada all helped to build the station.

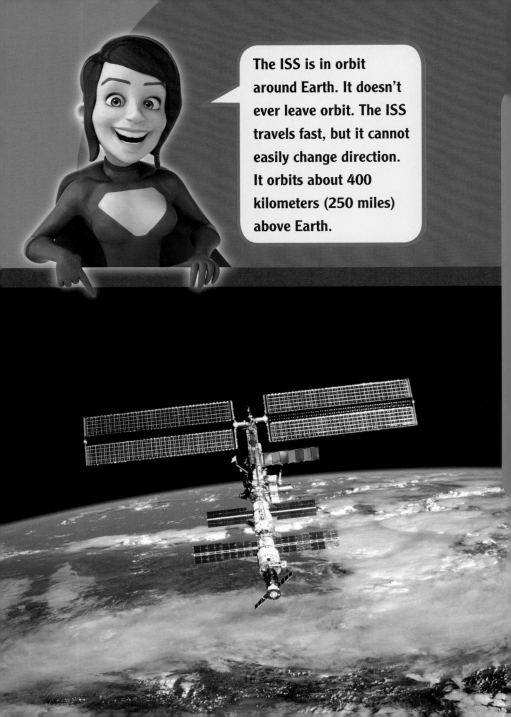

The ISS is in orbit around Earth. It doesn't ever leave orbit. The ISS travels fast, but it cannot easily change direction. It orbits about 400 kilometers (250 miles) above Earth.

Where is the ISS?

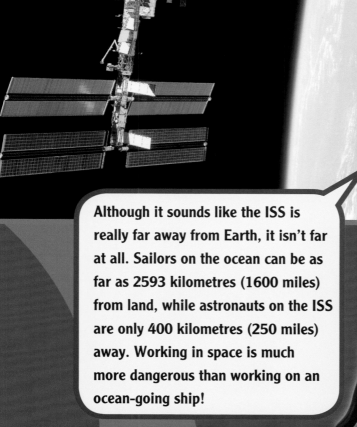

Although it sounds like the ISS is really far away from Earth, it isn't far at all. Sailors on the ocean can be as far as 2593 kilometres (1600 miles) from land, while astronauts on the ISS are only 400 kilometres (250 miles) away. Working in space is much more dangerous than working on an ocean-going ship!

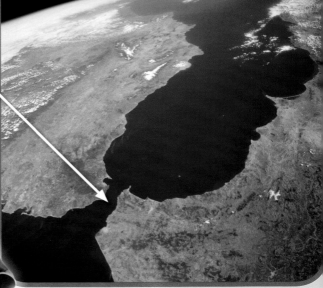

The Strait of Gibraltar (between Spain and Morocco)

Astronauts aboard the ISS take many photos of Earth. From the ISS, astronauts can see the spherical shape of the Earth. They can also see continents, lakes, oceans, mountains and cloud formations in great detail.

Earth from the ISS

Aurora Borealis (Northern Lights)

Hurricane

The Great Lakes (Canada and the U.S.)

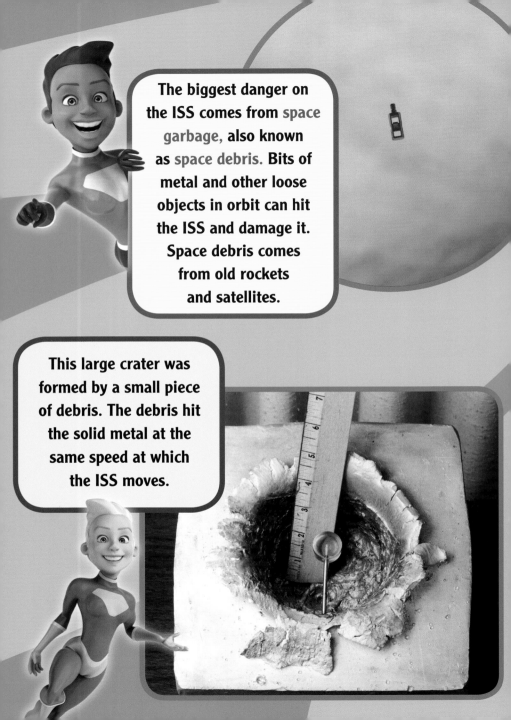

The biggest danger on the ISS comes from space garbage, also known as space debris. Bits of metal and other loose objects in orbit can hit the ISS and damage it. Space debris comes from old rockets and satellites.

This large crater was formed by a small piece of debris. The debris hit the solid metal at the same speed at which the ISS moves.

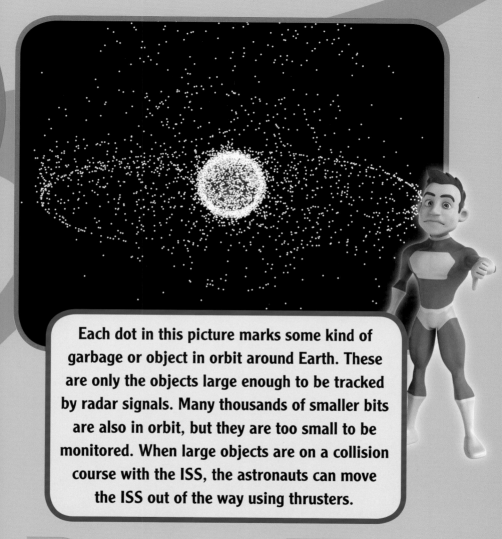

Each dot in this picture marks some kind of garbage or object in orbit around Earth. These are only the objects large enough to be tracked by radar signals. Many thousands of smaller bits are also in orbit, but they are too small to be monitored. When large objects are on a collision course with the ISS, the astronauts can move the ISS out of the way using thrusters.

Dangers Aboard the ISS

Zooming Around Earth

The ISS moves around Earth at a fast speed. It travels at more than 25,000 kilometers per hour (15,000 miles per hour)! That's more than 20 times the speed of sound!

The ISS completes a full orbit every 90 minutes. Astronauts aboard the ISS see 16 sunrises and 16 sunsets every 24 hours!

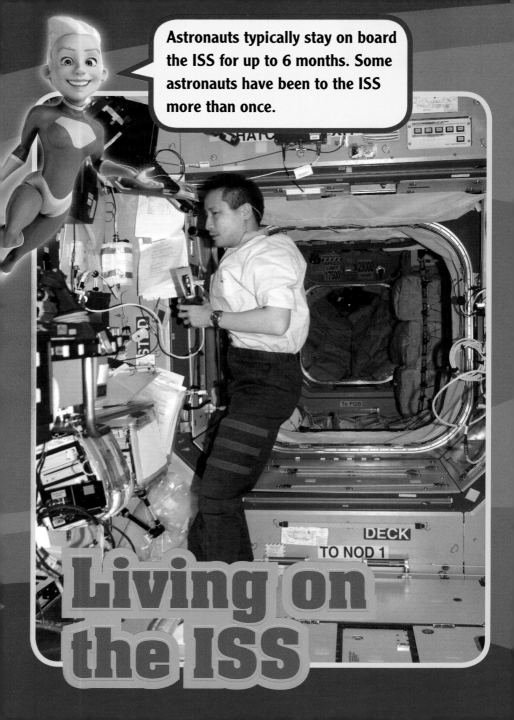

Astronauts typically stay on board the ISS for up to 6 months. Some astronauts have been to the ISS more than once.

Living on the ISS

The ISS has special machines to keep the environment safe for the astronauts. Machines keep the air clean and pressurized, produce oxygen, filter waste water into drinking water and monitor for fires.

Part of an astronaut's daily job is to maintain the equipment and machines on the ISS. The main part of their job is to conduct scientific research.

Robonaut

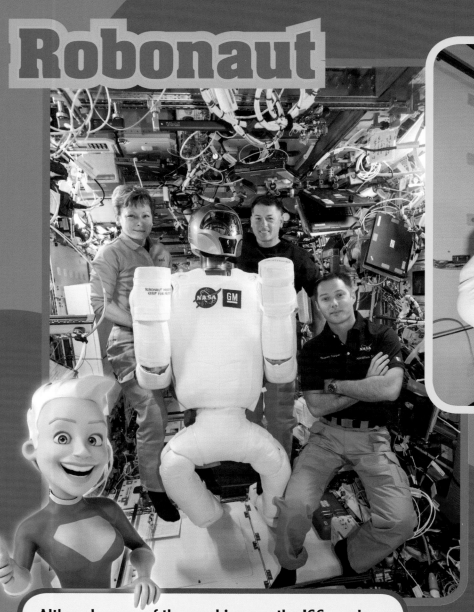

Although many of the machines on the ISS can be called robots, Robonaut is the only humanoid robot onboard. Robonaut was made to work with people.

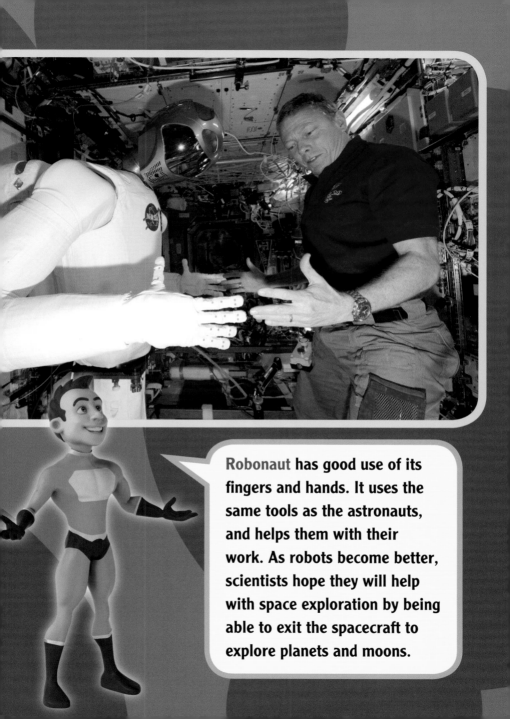

Robonaut has good use of its fingers and hands. It uses the same tools as the astronauts, and helps them with their work. As robots become better, scientists hope they will help with space exploration by being able to exit the spacecraft to explore planets and moons.

The astronauts aboard the ISS always stay in communication with their Flight Control Team.

A Flight Control Team monitors the ISS and its crew from NASA's Johnson Space Center in Houston.

Communication

The Flight Control Team is made up of various kinds of engineers who monitor the systems on the spacecraft. The Flight Director is in constant communication with the ISS. A Flight Surgeon monitors the health of each crew member.

Spacesuits

Astronauts wear 2 types of spacesuits. Their orange spacesuits are for flights to and from space. These suits are not pressurized. Astronauts cannot wear them outside the spacecraft in space. They are orange so that it is easy to see each other.

Astronauts also have white spacesuits that allow them to go outside the spacecraft into open space. These suits are pressurized with breathable air and are temperature controlled. Spacesuits also have communication systems built into them so the astronauts can communicate with their team inside the ISS.

Spacewalk

A spacewalk is any activity done by an astronaut outside of their spacecraft. Astronauts wear their white pressurized spacesuits to protect them in space. Spacewalks are also called Extravehicular Activities (EVAs).

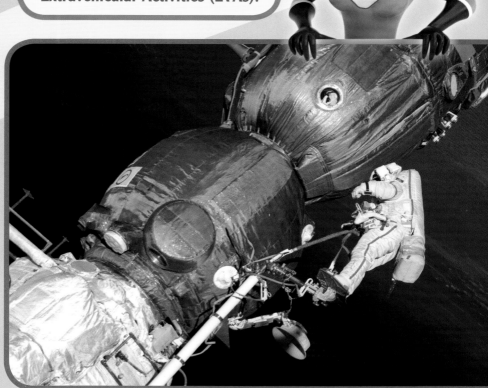

Astronauts perform spacewalks mainly to repair equipment or build new equipment on their spacecraft. For safety, the astronaut is tethered to the spacecraft.

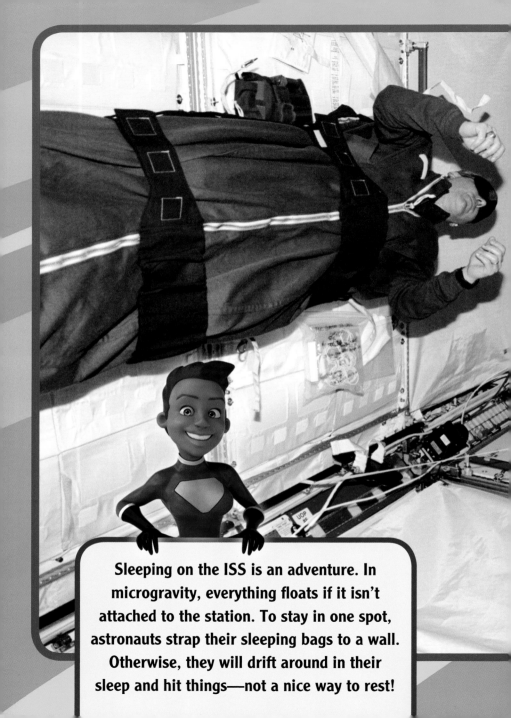

Sleeping on the ISS is an adventure. In microgravity, everything floats if it isn't attached to the station. To stay in one spot, astronauts strap their sleeping bags to a wall. Otherwise, they will drift around in their sleep and hit things—not a nice way to rest!

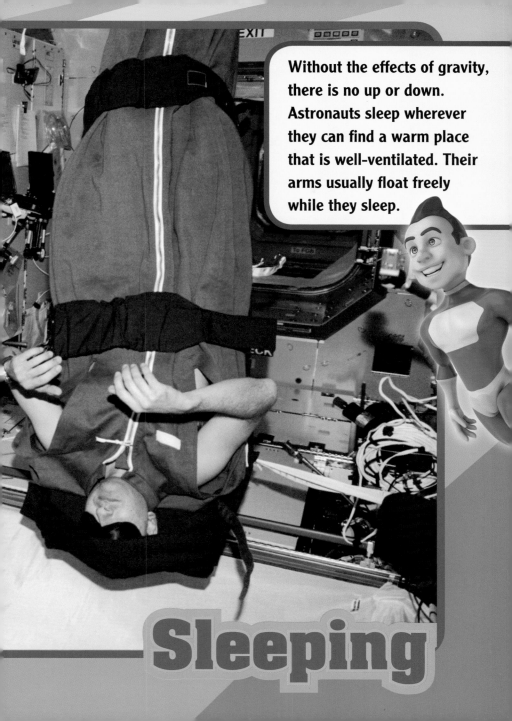

Without the effects of gravity, there is no up or down. Astronauts sleep wherever they can find a warm place that is well-ventilated. Their arms usually float freely while they sleep.

Sleeping

Floating food

Floating water

Eating & Drinking

Water is stored in large pouches. To drink water, astronauts open a small pouch and suck the water out.

In the galley where they eat, astronauts use a small vacuum to suck up any food crumbs or liquid droplets. Loose particles could get into the equipment or the ventilation system and cause problems!

To use the space toilet, astronauts have to buckle themselves onto it so they don't float off. The toilet doesn't flush. Instead, suction takes the waste away.

Toilets

On the ISS, everything is recycled. Liquid waste is recycled, but solid waste is dried, stored and returned to Earth.

In microgravity, astronauts have to exercise everyday. Without exercise, their muscles and bones would weaken from the feeling of weightlessness in space.

Exercise

Because everything and everyone floats in space, astronauts have to strap themselves onto the exercise machines to do a workout. Exercise helps keep them strong for when they return to Earth.

Keeping Clean

Washing hair is space is hard! Astronauts can only use a little bit of water and shampoo to wash their hair. They cannot rinse their hair in space, so they use a towel to soak up the water and shampoo.

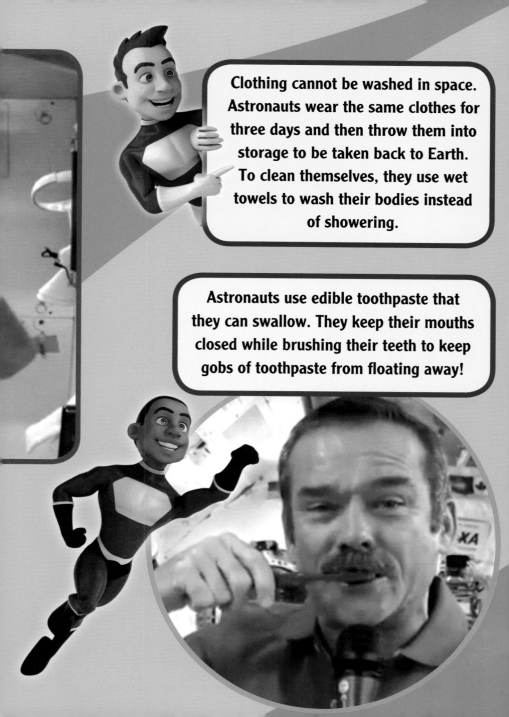

Clothing cannot be washed in space. Astronauts wear the same clothes for three days and then throw them into storage to be taken back to Earth. To clean themselves, they use wet towels to wash their bodies instead of showering.

Astronauts use edible toothpaste that they can swallow. They keep their mouths closed while brushing their teeth to keep gobs of toothpaste from floating away!

Free Time

Music is a popular free time activity aboard the ISS. There are several musical instruments on board, including a keyboard and a few guitars.

Astronauts can do other activities in their free time:

- write emails to friends and family
- watch movies
- take photos

The view of the Earth from the ISS is spectacular. Many amazing photos have been taken by astronauts.

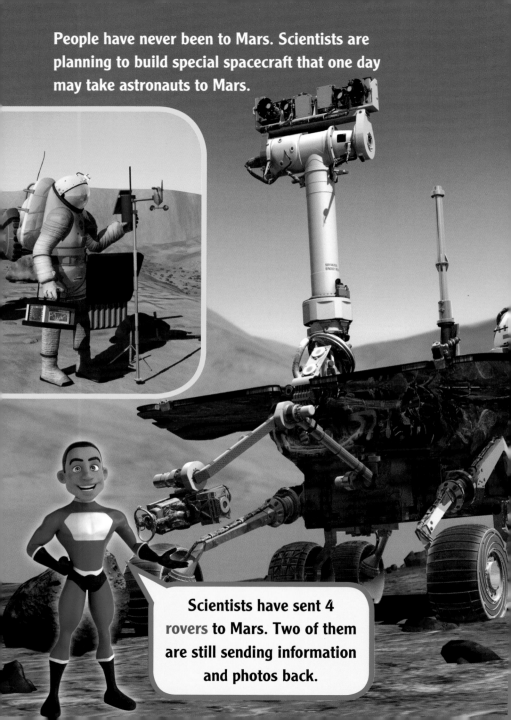

People have never been to Mars. Scientists are planning to build special spacecraft that one day may take astronauts to Mars.

Scientists have sent 4 **rovers** to Mars. Two of them are still sending information and photos back.

This is a photo of the Mars landscape taken by one of the rovers. The surface of Mars looks like a rocky desert. The rocks have lots of iron, so the planet looks red. People often call Mars the Red Planet.

Mars Missions

Beyond Mars

People traveling to Mars is still a dream. To travel beyond Mars is even more difficult to imagine. People think about traveling beyond Mars for two reasons. As we study space, we look for signs of life, especially intelligent life. Finding and meeting extra-terrestrial life is a dream for many scientists and space explorers.

In 1969, astronaut Neil Armstrong was the first person to walk on the moon. He was with astronaut Buzz Aldrin, who was the second person to walk on the moon.

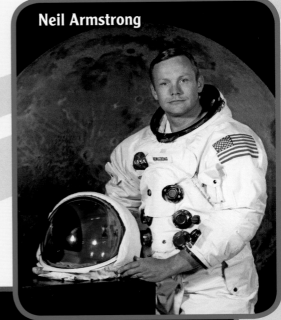

Neil Armstrong

Buzz Aldrin

Famous Astronauts

Gennady Padalka is a Russian cosmonaut. He has spent more time in space than any other astronaut. When he retired, he had spent 879 days in space. That's two and a half years!

Gennady Padalka

More Famous Astronauts

Chris Hadfield is a Canadian astronaut who was the the first Canadian commander of the ISS. He was also the first Canadian to spacewalk.

Chris Hadfield

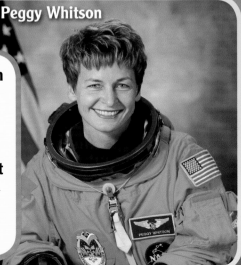

Peggy Whitson

Peggy Whitson is an American astronaut who has spent 665 days in 3 missions on the ISS. This is the most for any female astronaut and the most for any American astronaut. She was also the first female commander of the ISS.

Jim Voss

While serving on the ISS, astronauts Jim Voss and Susan Helms conducted an 8-hour and 56-minute spacewalk. That's the world record!

Susan Helms

The Publisher: Super Explorers is an imprint of Blue Bike Books

Library and Archives Canada Cataloguing in Publication

Title: Astronauts and space / Tamara Hartson.

Names: Hartson, Tamara, 1974– author.

Identifiers: Canadiana (print) 20190179872 | Canadiana (ebook) 20190179902 | ISBN 9781897278932 (softcover) | ISBN 9781897278956 (EPUB)

Subjects: LCSH: Astronauts—Juvenile literature. | LCSH: Astronauts—Biography—Juvenile literature. | LCSH: Manned space flight—Juvenile literature.

Classification: LCC TL793 .H37 2019 | DDC j629.450092—dc23

Front cover credit: Spacewalk, NASA.

Back cover credits: From NASA/ESA: a, c; from Wikimedia Commons: Teknoraver, b.

Photo Credits: All photos are courtesy of NASA/ESA except for the following: Getty Images: RomoloTavani, 6-7. Wikimedia Commons: Concierge.2C, 11; Teknoraver, 8, 9.

Superhero Illustrations: julos/Thinkstock.

Produced with the assistance of the Government of Alberta. Alberta Government

We acknowledge the financial support of the Government of Canada.

Nous reconnaissons l'appui financier du gouvernement du Canada.

Funded by the Government of Canada
Financé par le gouvernement du Canada | Canadä

PC: 38